Dedicated

To

All the Past & Present Judges of the Supreme Court of India.

Salute to their wisdom.

Salute to their interpretation of Law.

Salute to their elaborative judgement writing.

INSIDER TRADING AND MARKET MANIPULATION- SEBI ACT- SUPREME COURT'S LEADING CASE LAWS

CASE NOTES- FACTS- FINDINGS OF APEX COURT JUDGES & CITATIONS

JAYPRAKASH BANSILAL SOMANI

Contents

Contents

Preface

Dear Learned Advocates of the SEBI Tribunals, High Courts, Supreme Court, Corporates & Individuals

I am very delighted to provide you a book on 'INSIDER TRADING AND MARKET MANIPULATION- SEBI ACT'- Supreme Court of India's Leading Case Laws'.

In this book you will get...

1. Name of the Case i. e. Cause title

2.Relevant Sections discussed in the case

3. Hon'ble Judges/Coram of the case

4.Number of PDF Pages in Original Judgement of the case

5. All available Citations of the case

6. Case Note with appeal allowed/ dismissed or disposed off

7. Facts of the case

8. Hon'ble Apex Court's findings, while dismissing/allowing or disposing the appeal

9. Ratio Decidendi if any.

My special thanks to Manupatra, because of their web portal I can compile this book in well manner. I am also thankful to Notion Press to support me to publish & market this book throughout the Country. Thanks to my Juniors, Advocate Colleagues & Insolvency Professional Colleagues to support me in this venture.

Mr Rachit Manchanda has helped me a lot to compile this book.

I hope this book will add some value addition in the wealth of your legal knowledge. Your positive feedbacks will boost me to compile/ write further books & negative feedbacks will improve my skills. Kindly send your valuable feedbacks by email.

Thanks with Regards,

Jayprakash B. Somani

Advocate, Supreme Court of India

Email: jaysomani64@gmail.com

Web Site:www.jayprakashsomani.com

Call: 8384051134, 9322188701, 9318381287

Acknowledgements

Printed & Published by
Notion Press
No. 8, 3rd Cross Street,
CIT Colony, Mylapore,
Chennai, Tamil Nadu- 600004

Managed by
Jayprakash Somani Advocates & Solicitors
Law Firm for Supreme Court of India
Delhi Office
257 C, Pocket 1, Mayur Vihar Phase 1, Delhi 110091.
Call 8384051134, 9322188701, 8459194576, 9318381287 01141051516
Supreme Court Chamber
312, 3rd Floor, M. C. Setalvad Block, In front of 'D' Gate, Bhagwan Das Road, Supreme Court of India, New Delhi 110001
Contact: 8459194576, 9811011747,
www.jayprakashsomani.com

Books are available online at
1. Notion Press: https://notionpress.com/author/jayprakash_somani
2. Amazon: https://www.amazon.in/s?k=jayprakash+somani
3. Flipkart: https://www.flipkart.com/search?q=Jayprakash%20Somani

I

Siddharth Chaturvedi and Ors. Vs. Securities and Exchange Board of India, 2016

Hon'ble Judges/Coram: *Kurian Joseph and Rohinton Fali Nariman, JJ*

Relevant sections:

Securities And Exchange Board Of India Act, 1992 - Section 15A; Securities And Exchange Board Of India Act, 1992 - Section 15J

Equivalent Citation:

[2016]132CLA149(SC), [2016]195CompCas516(SC), (2019)3CompLJ20(SC), (2016)3MLJ75, 2016(3)SCALE417, (2016)12SCC119, 2016 (6) SCJ 304, [2016]135SCL106(SC), MANU/SC/0321/2016

No of pages in judgment: 6

Case Notes:

Capital Market - Violation of Regulations - Imposition of penalty - Substantiality thereof - Sections 15A and 15J of Securities and Exchange Board of India Act, 1992 - Appellants purchased shares - Show cause notice issued for violation of Securities and Exchange Board of India (Prohibition of Insider Trading) Regulations, 1992 - Penalty imposed by Adjudicating Officer - Appeal before Tribunal dismissed - Hence, present Appeal - Whether penalty on Appellant was rightly imposed in view of Section 15A of Act, 1992, as amended in year 2002 - Whether Adjudicating Officer had properly considered factors under Section 15J of Act, 1992 before imposing penalty

Brief facts:

The Appellants made certain purchases of shares of the Brijlaxmi Leasing and Finance Company. A show cause notice came to be issued by the Respondent SEBI to the Appellant Under Rule 4(1) of the Securities and Exchange Board of India (Procedure for holding inquiry and imposing penalty by adjudicating officer) Rules, 1995 for the alleged violation of the provisions of Regulations 13(4), 13(4A) and 13(5) of the Securities and Exchange Board of India (Prohibition of Insider Trading) Regulations, 1992.

The Adjudicating Officer, by various orders imposed a penalty of Rs. 5 lacs, 7 lacs and 11 lacs respectively, in the three civil appeals, before us. An appeal made to the Securities Appellate Tribunal suffered the same fate, and was dismissed by the Tribunal stating that there is no dispute that there was violation of mandatory Regulations, and that in any case, a penalty of Rs. one crore could have been imposed on facts, whereas, in fact, the Adjudicating Officer penalised the Appellants with a penalty of Rs. 5 lacs, 7 lacs and 11 lacs respectively, which cannot be said to be excessively harsh or unreasonable.

Held, while referring the matter to the larger Bench,

These appeals raise an interesting question of the interplay between Section 15A, as amended in the year 2002, and Section 15J of the Securities and Exchange Board of India Act, 1992 (in short 'the SEBI Act').

Penalty for failure to furnish information, return, etc.-If any person, who is required under this Act or any rules or Regulations made thereunder:

a. to furnish any document, return or report to the Board, fails to furnish the same, he shall be liable to a penalty which shall not be less than one lakh rupees but which may extend to one lakh rupees for each day during which such failure continues subject to a maximum of one crore rupees;

The purpose of amendment was clearly to reintroduce the discretion of the adjudicating Officer which was taken away by the SEBI (Amendment) Act, 2002. Had the failure of the Respondent taken place between 29.10.2002 and 8.9.2014, the penalty ought to have been Rs. 1 crore, without the possibility of any discretion for reduction.

Two things have been clearly stated by this Court in so far as the amended Section 15A read with Section 15J is concerned. First, this Court has indicated that by the use of the expression "namely" in Section 15J, SEBI in adjudging the quantum of penalty Under Section 15A can have due regard only to the three factors set out therein and not to other relevant factors as the expression "namely" cannot be equated with the expression "including", being an exhaustive provision on the subject matter covered by the provision. This Court has also clearly held that Section 15J would suffer an eclipse for the period 2002 to 2014 inasmuch as the intention of the Legislature, by amending Section 15A, seems to be that no scope for any discretion for this period is to be exercised, if in fact, there is any infraction of Rules or Regulations. This Court clearly held that the discretionary power of the Adjudicating Officer having been withdrawn, the scope of Section 15J would correspondingly stand drastically reduced.

Prima facie, we find it a little difficult to subscribe to both the views contained in paragraph 4 as well as in paragraph 5 of the said judgment. The expression "shall have due regard to" is a very known legislative device used from the time of *Julius* v. *Bishop of Oxford* (1880) LR 5 AC 214 (HL), and followed in many judgments both English as well as of our Courts as words vesting a discretion in an Adjudicating Officer. The question which arises in the present appeals is whether the expression "namely" fixes the discretion which can be exercised only in the circumstances mentioned in the three clauses set out in Section 15J, or whether it would also take into account other relevant circumstances, having particular regard to the fact that it is a penalty provision that the Court is construing. As this needs to be authoritatively decided for the future, it would be better if we refer it to a larger Bench for such authoritative pronouncement.

Interim orders passed by this Court shall continue to operate.

II

Securities and Exchange Board of India Vs. Kishore R. Ajmera, 2016

Hon'ble Judges/Coram: *Ranjan Gogoi and Prafulla C. Pant, JJ.*

Relevant Sections:

SECURITIES AND EXCHANGE BOARD OF INDIA ACT, 1992 - Section 15J

Equivalent Citation: AIR2016SC1079, 2016(2)BomCR713, [2016]131CLA187(SC), [2016]196CompCas181(SC), (2016)3CompLJ198(SC), 2016(2)SCALE511, (2016)6SCC368, 2016 (5) SCJ 517, [2016]134SCL481(SC), (2016)6WBLR(SC)522, MANU/SC/0192/2016

Case Note:

Capital Market – Fraudulent activities - Involvement therein - Degree of proof - Brokers/sub-brokers found indulged in fraudulent/manipulative practices -Tribunal set aside charges and penalty for lack of evidence - Hence, present Appeals - Whether degree of proof was sufficient enough for deciding indulgence of Brokers/Sub-brokers in fraudulent practices

Brief Facts:

The core question of law arising in this group of appeals being similar and the facts involved being largely identical, all the appeals which were heard analogously are being decided by this common order. The question of law arising in this group of appeals may be summarized as follows What is the degree of proof required to hold brokers/sub-brokers liable for fraudulent/manipulative practices under the Securities and Exchange

Board of India (Prohibition of Fraudulent and Unfair Trade Practices Relating to Securities Market) Regulations and/or liable for violating the Code of Conduct specified in Schedule II read with Regulation 9 of the Securities and Exchange Board of India (Stock Broker and Sub-Brokers) Regulations,1992?

Held while dismissing the appeal:

In the light of the above discussions, we dismiss the Civil Appeal No. 2818 of 2008 (SEBI v. Kishore R. Ajmera) and affirm the order dated 05.02.2008 passed by the Securities Appellate Tribunal, Mumbai.

Insofar as the remaining appeals are concerned, we allow the same and set aside the orders of the Securities Appellate Tribunal, Mumbai passed in each of the appeals and restore the orders and penalty imposed on the Respondents-brokers by the respective orders of the Whole Time Member of the SEBI.

III

B.S.E. Brokers Forum, Bombay and Ors. vs. Securities and Exchange Board of India and Ors., 2001

Hon'ble Judges/Coram: *B.N. Kirpal, N. Santosh Hegde and Brijesh Kumar, JJ.*

Relevant Section:

Securities and Exchange Board of India Act, 1992 - Section 3

Equivalent Citation: AIR2001SC1010, [2001]40CLA258(SC), [2001]104CompCas506(SC), (2001)1CompLJ193(SC), JT2001(2)SC242, 2001(1)SCALE575, (2001)3SCC482, MANU/SC/0069/2001

Case Note:

Company- member - Chapter 5 of National Stock Exchange Bye-laws, Section 3 of Securities Contracts (Regulation) Act, 1956 and Regulation 10 of Securities and Exchange Board of India (Stock brokers and Sub-brokers) Rules, 1992 - validity of Regulation 10 questioned - Section 3 (2) (c) requires stock exchange applying for recognition to specify various classes of members to be admitted as members of stock exchange - no distinction made between full fledged member and trading member of National Stock

Exchange (NSE) - definition of trading member under NSE Bye-laws shows that trading member to be stock broker and member of NSE - he must be registered in accordance with chapter 5 - trading member mean member of stock exchange - Explanation clarifies that more than one class of trading members of exchange may be determined by board from time to time - trading member need not necessarily be member of NSE - held, there can be more than one class of members who can be admitted as members of stock exchange and any of those members belonging to any of those classes will fall within definition of member - Regulation 10 validly applicable to members.

Held while dismissing the appeal,

A trading member of the NSE need not necessarily be a member of the company that is NSE. Therefore, it is clear from the Articles of NSE that the said Exchange itself recognises a trading member to be a member of the Stock Exchange though with limited rights. Therefore, it is clear that there can be more than one class of members who can be admitted as members of the stock exchange and any of those members belonging to any of those classes so long as they are registered as such by a stock exchange, will fall within the definition of 'member' as defined in Section 2 © of the SCR Act and Rule 2(e) of the SEBI Rules. It is also undisputed that the trading members of the NSE are carrying on the business of stock brokering, hence, keeping in mind the objects of the Act, it would be futile to contend that the trading members of the NSE cannot be considered to be the stock brokers for the limited purpose of the liability to pay the impugned fee under the Act, Rules and Regulations. Therefore, this contention also should fail.

For the reasons stated above and subject to the directions issued by us in regard to the implementation of the Bhatt Committee Report, T.C. © No. 20/2000 fails and the same is hereby dismissed.

WP © No. 502/2000 :

In view of the order passed in T.C. © No. 20/2000 hereinabove, this petition is also dismissed.

IV

N Narayanan vs. Adjudicating Officer, SEBI, 2013

Hon'ble Judges: *K.S. Panicker Radhakrishnan and Dipak Misra, JJ.*

RelevantSections: 15Z OF SECURITIES AND EXCHANGE BOARD OF INDIA ACT, 1992

Equivalent Citation: 2013(4)ABR889, 2013VII AD (S.C.) 162, AIR2013SC3191, 2013(3)ALLMR973, 2013(4)BomCR61, 2013 (2) CCC 157 , [2013]114CLA232(SC), [2013]178CompCas390(SC), (2013)3CompLJ45(SC), (2013)3CompLJ45(SC), JT2013(6)SC250, 2013-3-LW723, 2013(3)RCR(Civil)68, 2013(6)SCALE438, (2013)12SCC152, [2013]120SCL158(SC), MANU/SC/0426/2013

Case Note:

Capital Market - Imposition of Penalty - Section 15HA of Securities and Exchange Board of India Act, 1992 - Securities Appellate Tribunal, upholding order passed by SEBI restraining Appellant for a period of two years from buying, selling or dealing in securities and order passed by the adjudication officer imposing a monetary penalty of 50 lacs under Section 15HA of SEBI Act - Hence, this Appeal - Whether, Securities Appellate Tribunal was justified in upholding order passed by SEBI - Held, investigation had revealed that financial results contained in quarterly report filed with stock exchanges contained inflated figures of company's revenue profits, security deposits and receivables - Further, manipulation in financial results of company resulted in price rise of scrip of company and promoters pledged their shares to raise substantial funds from financial institutions - Thereby, Directors of company had "created artificiality" by projecting inflated figures of company's revenue, profits, security deposits and receivables - Therefore, conduct of Appellant and Ors. was, fraudulent and practices they had adopted, relating to securities, was unfair, which attracted penalty provisions contained in Section 15HA read with 15J of SEBI Act - Thus, SEBI had rightly restrained Appellant for a period of two years from date of that order from buying, selling or dealing with any securities, in any manner, or accessing securities market, directly or indirectly and from being Director of any listed company and that adjudicating officer had rightly imposed a penalty of Rs. 50 lakhs under Section 15HA of SEBI Act - Appeals dismissed.

Ratio Decidendi: "Company though a legal entity could not act by itself, it could act only through its Directors".

Brief facts:

The Appellant was the promoter as well as a whole time Director of M/s. Pyramid Saimira Theatre Limited (PSTL), a company registered under the Companies Act, 1956. The shares of PSTL were listed on Bombay Stock Exchange Ltd. (BSE) and National Stock Exchange (NSE) at the relevant time. The company was involved in the business of Exhibition (Theatre), Film and Television, Content Production, Distribution, Hospitality, Food & Beverage, Animation and Gaming and Cine Advertising etc. The company had nine Directors, including the Appellant herein. The investigation department of SEBI noticed that the company had committed serious irregularities in its books of accounts and showed inflated profits and revenues in the financial statements and lured the general public to invest in the shares of the company based on such false financial statements thereby violated the provisions of Securities and Exchange Board of India (Prohibition of Fraudulent and Unfair Trade Practice Relating to Securities Market) Regulations, 2003 (for short 'Regulations 2003'). Consequently, a notice was issued to the Appellant and to the other Directors stating that they had violated Section 12A of SEBI Act and Regulation 3(b), 3(c), 3(d), 4(1), 4(2)(a), 4(2)(e), 4(2) (f), 4(2)(k), 4(2)(r) of Regulations 2003 and were directed to show cause why appropriate directions as deemed fit and proper Under Sections 11, 11B and 11(4) of the SEBI Act read with Regulation 11 of Regulations 2003 be not issued against them.

The Appellant submitted a detailed reply stating that it was the Managing Director and Principal Officer of the company who was in charge of day-to-day affairs of the company including the operations, finance and accounts, secretarial and compliance, legal services and technical services. Appellant, it was stated, though was a whole time Director of the company was only handling Human Resource Department of the company and was fully engrossed in the recruitment of personnel, training and team buildup. Further, it was also stated that he had only relied upon the auditor's statements in financial matters and hence was not personally liable for the violation of the provisions of SEBI Act and Regulations 2003. Personal hearing was accorded to the Appellant on 30.8.2010. Written Submissions dated 15.9.2010 filed by the Appellant was also considered by SEBI. The Board noticed following specific violations:

(a) manipulated accounts by fictitious entries;

(b) made false disclosures to the stock exchange;

(c) did not co-operate with the investigations, and

(d) did not maintain certain books of accounts.

7. The Adjudicating Officer also held that the Appellant and Ors. have violated the provisions of Section 12A of SEBI Act and Regulation 3(b), 3(c), 3(d), 4(1), 4(2)(a), 4(2)(e), 4(2)(f), 4(2)(k), 4(2)(r) of Regulations 2003 and took the view that the Appellant and other Directors are liable for monetary penalty Under Section 15HA of SEBI Act whereby a penalty of 50 lacs was imposed on the Appellant.

Held while dismissing the appeal,

Conduct of Appellant and Ors. was, fraudulent and practices they had adopted, relating to securities, was unfair, which attracted penalty provisions contained in Section 15HA read with 15J of SEBI Act - Thus, SEBI had rightly restrained Appellant for a period of two years from date of that order from buying, selling or dealing with any securities, in any manner, or accessing securities market, directly or indirectly and from being Director of any listed company and that adjudicating officer had rightly imposed a penalty of Rs. 50 lakhs under Section 15HA of SEBI Act - Appeals dismissed.

V

Vijay Kumar Jain vs. Standard Chartered Bank and Ors., 2019

Hon'ble Judges/Coram: *Rohinton Fali Nariman and Navin Sinha, JJ.*

Relevant Sections: 15Z OF SECURITIES AND EXCHANGE BOARD OF INDIA ACT, 1992

Equivalent Citation: AIR2019SC2477, I(2019)BC482(SC), 2019 (1) CCC 402 , [2019]148CLA542(SC), (2020)4CompLJ441(SC), 123(1)CWN347, 2019(1)RCR(Civil)865, 2019(2)SCALE352, 2019 (8) SCJ 658, [2019]152SCL56(SC), MANU/SC/0111/2019

Case Notes:

Company - Resolution plans - Committee of creditors - Right to participate - Meetings - Sections 21, 25, 30 of Insolvency and Bankruptcy Code, 2016; Regulations 25, 34, 38 of Insolvency and Bankruptcy Board of India (Insolvency Resolution Process for Corporate Persons) Regulations, 2016 [CIRP Regulations] - Present appeal arose out of an Appellate Tribunal's judgment rejecting Appellant's prayer for directions to resolution professional to provide all relevant documents including insolvency resolution plans in question to members of suspended Board of Directors of corporate debtor in each case so that, they might meaningfully participate in meetings held by committee of creditors [CoC] - Whether Appellate Tribunal which recognized Appellant's right to attend and participate in CoC meetings, but denied Appellant's prayer to access certain documents, most particularly, resolution plans was sustainable.

Brief Facts:

Ruchi Soya Industries Ltd.- corporate debtor, was incorporated on 6th January, 1986. It was said to be a profit-making company in business of processing of oil-seeds and refining crude oil for edible use. In September, 2017, Company Petition were filed by Standard Chartered Bank Ltd. and DBS Bank Ltd., being financial creditors of aforesaid corporate debtor. These two company petitions were admitted on 8th and 15th December, 2017, respectively, by National Company Law Tribunal [NCLT]. One Shri Shailendra Ajmera of Ernst and Young was appointed as Interim Resolution Professional in both petitions. CoC was constituted under Section 21 of Insolvency and Bankruptcy Code, 2016 [Insolvency Code], and Appellant being a member of suspended Board of Directors was given notice and agenda for first CoC meeting held on 12th January, 2018, and was permitted to attend aforesaid meeting. He alleged, which was disputed by Respondents, that subsequent meetings of CoC were held in which he was denied participation. Appellant filed Miscellaneous Application before NCLT in order that, Appellant be allowed to effectively participate in these meetings. In tenth meeting dated 12th August, 2018, Appellant executed a nondisclosure agreement for sharing resolution plans of corporate debtor. Under said agreement, Appellant undertook to indemnify resolution professional and keep information that was received as to resolution plan strictly confidential. NCLT dismissed application with liberty to Appellant to attend CoC meetings but not to insist upon being provided information considered confidential either by resolution professional or committee of creditors. Against this order, Appellant filed an appeal before Appellate Tribunal which recognized Appellant's right to attend and participate in CoC meetings, but denied Appellant's prayer to access certain documents, most particularly, resolution plans. Thereafter, an application for modification/ clarification of Appellate Tribunal's order was also dismissed. Aggrieved by order of Appellate Tribunal, Appellants had filed present appeal.

Held, while allowing the appeal,

Statutory scheme of Insolvency and Bankruptcy Code, 2016 made it clear that though erstwhile Board of Directors were not members of committee of creditors, yet, they had a right to participate in each and every meeting held by committee of creditors, and also had a right to discuss along with members of committee of creditors all resolution plans that were presented at such meetings under Section 25(2)(i). Operational creditors, who might participate in such meetings but had no right to vote, were vitally interested in such resolution plans, and must be furnished copies of such plans beforehand if they were to participate effectively in meeting of committee of creditors. Under Section 30(2)(b), repayment of their debts was an important part of resolution plan qua them on which they must comment. Even though persons such as operational creditors had no right to vote but were only participants in meetings of committee of creditors, yet, they would certainly had a right to be given a copy of resolution plans before such meetings were held so that they might effectively comment on same to safeguard their interest. [9] 2. Every participant was entitled to a notice of every meeting of committee of creditors. Such notice of meeting must contain an agenda of meeting, together with copies of all documents relevant for matters to be discussed and issues to be voted upon at meeting vide Regulation 21(3)(iii). Obviously, resolution plans were "matters to be discussed" at such meetings, and erstwhile Board of Directors were "participants" who would discuss these issues. Expression "documents" was a wide expression which would certainly include resolution plans. [13] 3. Under Regulation 24(2)(e), resolution professional had to take a roll call of every participant attending through video conferencing or other audio and visual means, and must state for record that such person had received agenda and all relevant material for meeting which would include resolution plan to be discussed at such meeting. Regulation 35 made it clear that, resolution professional shall provide fair value and liquidation value to every member of the committee only after receipt of resolution plans in accordance with Code. Also, under Regulation 38(1)(a), a resolution plan shall include a statement as to how it had dealt with interest of all stakeholders, and under Sub-clause 3(a), a resolution plan shall demonstrate that, it addressed cause of default. This Regulation also, therefore, recognized vital interest of erstwhile Board of Directors in a resolution plan together with cause of default. Erstwhile directors could represent to committee of creditors that, cause of default was not due to erstwhile management, but due to other factors which might be beyond their control, which had led to non-payment of debt. Therefore, a combined reading of Code as well as Regulations led to conclusion that, members of erstwhile Board of Directors, being vitally interested in resolution plans that might be discussed at meetings of committee of creditors, must be given a copy of such plans as part of "documents" that had to be furnished along with notice of such meetings. [14] 4. Regarding confidential information was concerned, it was clear that, resolution professional could take an undertaking from members of erstwhile Board of Directors, as had been taken in facts of present case, to maintain confidentiality. Source of this power was Regulation 7(2)(h) of Insolvency and Bankruptcy Board of India (Insolvency Professionals) Regulations, 2016, read with paragraph 21 of First Schedule thereto. This could be in form of a non-disclosure agreement in which resolution professional could be indemnified in case information was not kept strictly confidential. [15] 5. Proviso to Section 21(2) clarified that, a director who was also a financial creditor who was a related party of corporate debtor shall not have any right of representation, participation, or voting in a meeting of committee of creditors. Directors, simplicitor, were not subject matter of proviso to Section 21(2), but only directors who were related parties of corporate debtor. It was only such persons who did not have any right of representation, participation, or voting in a meeting of committee of creditors. Therefore, contention that a director simplicitor would have right to get documents as against a director who was a financial creditor was not an argument that was based on proviso to Section 21(2), correctly read, as it referred only to a financial creditor who was a related party of corporate debtor. [16] 6. Time that had been utilized in present proceedings must be excluded from period of resolution process of corporate debtor as had been held in Arcelormittal India Private Limited v. Satish Kumar Gupta and Ors. Appellants would be given copies of all resolution plans submitted to CoC within a period of two weeks from date of this judgment. Resolution applicant in each of these cases would then convene a meeting of CoC within two weeks thereafter, which would include Appellants as participants. CoC would then deliberate on resolution plans afresh and either reject them or approve of them with requisite majority, after which, further procedure detailed in the Code and Regulations would be followed. NCLAT judgment was set aside. Appeal allowed. [18]

VI

Securities and Exchange Board of India Vs. PAN Asia Advisors ltd and Ors., 2015

Relevant Sections:

Securities And Exchange Board Of India Act, 1992 - Rule 11B; Securities And Exchange Board Of India Act, 1992 - Rule 12; Securities And Exchange Board Of India Act, 1992 - Rule 12A; Securities And Exchange Board Of India Act, 1992 - Rule 11C

Equivalent Citation:

AIR2015SC2782, III(2015)BC513(SC), 2015 (3) CCC 120 , [2015]127CLA306(SC), [2015]191CompCas410(SC), (2015)3CompLJ241(SC), 2015(7)SCALE694, (2015)14SCC71, 2015 (8) SCJ 437, [2016]134SCL311(SC), MANU/SC/0761/2015

Case Notes:

Capital Market - Access to market - To debar - Jurisdiction - SEBI had debarred Respondent from accessing capital market, on ground of fraud in GDR process - Whether SEBI had jurisdiction to initiate proceedings against Lead Managers, on ground of fraud committed at issue of GDR process outside India - Whether SEBI had jurisdiction to debar access to capital market for period of ten years.

Brief Facts:

The Respondent company had issued equity shares of Rs. 29,91,00,000/- of Rupee one each at the value of 2 USD. Such shares issued resulted in allotment of 29,91,000 GDRs containing 29,91,00,000 equity shares. The total value of the GDRs issued was 5.98 million USD. Such GDRs issued were fully subscribed and closed on 29.04.2009 itself. Prior to the GDRs issue, Asahi had 3,71,96,000 fully paid equity shares and GDRs issued was about eight times of its outstanding share capital. The Respondent no. 1 was appointed as the Lead Manager for the GDR issued and the entirety of the share capital of the Respondent no. 1 was held by the Respondent no. 2. At the instance of SEBI that there was a loan taken from Euram by Vintage for subscribing to the GDRs of Respondent and that the same was managed by a loan and pledge agreement signed not only by Vintage and Euram but by Respondent as well. According to SEBI, the Respondent structured the loan and pledge agreement to which the Respondent company, Vintage and Euram were signatories and the terms of the loan agreement as well as the pledge agreement were intertwined and they were the keys to the alleged fraudulent issuance and subscription of GDRs.

Held while allowing the appeal:

In the light of the features noted and alleged by SEBI as against the Respondents, relating to GDRs issued by the six entities for whom the Respondents acted as Lead Manager, with particular reference to the extent of the involvement of the Respondents even while acting as Lead Managers, while facilitating the issuing companies in the fixation of price of the GDRs and its trading in the global market, according to SEBI, by virtue of such fraudulent nature of involvement of the Respondents along with the issuing company, SEBI is entitled to invoke its jurisdiction u/s 11, 11B, 11C, 12 & 12A of SEBI Act, 1992 read along with its 2003 Regulations and consequently its order dated 20th June 2013 debarring the Respondents from rendering services in connection with the instruments which are defined as 'securities' u/s 2(h) of SCR Act, 1956 in the Indian market or dealing with them either directly or indirectly for a period of ten years from the date of its orders and also prohibiting them from getting access to the capital market directly or indirectly for the said period of ten years was justified. The definition of 'securities' u/s 2(h)(iii) of SCR Act, 1956 makes it clear that even if GDR as such is not specifically referred to under the definition of 'securities' u/s 2(h), any rights or interests in securities would also fall within the definition of securities. Viewed in that respect, every issue of GDR is based on the underlying shares of the issuing company deposited with the Domestic Custodian Bank which clearly falls under the definition of securities of Section 2(h), the GDR which create rights and interests in those securities, the GDR would automatically fall and come within the definition of Section 2(h) viz., 'securities'. [75] and[79]

This court is therefore convinced that having regard to the nature of allegations in the interests of investors in securities as well as the statutory obligation/duty cast upon SEBI to protect their interests, SEBI has got every jurisdiction to proceed against the Respondents as well as the issuing company.

As far as the stand of the second Respondent that he is a non-resident Indian residing in Dubai till September, 2011 and was the Managing Director of the first Respondent and that the first Respondent is a distinct and separate legal entity from the second Respondent and therefore the first Respondent cannot be made liable or responsible for the action of the second Respondent, it must be stated that even as per the legal opinion of M/s. Singhania and Co the Solicitors and Indian Advocates based at London who have stated apparently on the instructions of the second Respondent, that he was the sole shareholder of the first Respondent who is a non-resident Indian residing at Dubai. Therefore, it is too late in the day for the Respondents in attempting to get themselves excluded from the alleged violations as against the issuing companies along with the Respondents, which resulted in the passing of the order of debarment. This court therefore holds that SEBI had jurisdiction in passing the impugned order debarring the Respondents for a period of 10 years in dealing with the securities while considering the role played by the Respondents as Lead Managers relating to the GDRs issued by six companies which issued such GDRs. We, therefore, hold that the Tribunal is bound to examine the correctness or otherwise of the order of SEBI. [91] and[105].

VII

Securities and Exchange Board Vs. Classic Credit ltd, 2017

Relevant Sections:

SECURITIES AND EXCHANGE BOARD OF INDIA ACT, 1992 - Section 24; SECURITIES AND EXCHANGE BOARD OF INDIA ACT, 1992 - Section 26(2)

Equivalent Citation:

2017 (3) ALT (Crl.) 178 (A.P.), IV(2017)BC237(SC), III(2017)CCR436(SC), [2017]141CLA108(SC), (2017)4CompLJ34(SC), 2017(3)Crimes289(SC), 2017(9)SCALE458, (2018)13SCC1, 2017 (8) SCJ 510, [2017]143SCL422(SC), MANU/SC/1030/2017

Number of pages in the original judgement:3

Case Notes:

Capital Market - Forum of trial - Change thereof - Sections 24 and 26(2) of Securities and Exchange Board of India Act, 1992 - Complaints were filed against private parties, for offences punishable under Securities and Exchange Board of India Act, 1992 - Change of forum for trial, was assailed by some of private parties, before Court to which matters were committed - Their challenge failed - Matters were then carried, to High Court - Some of private parties, directly approached High Court, to assail changed forum of trial - High Court, through impugned judgment collectively disposed of all matters pending before it, by setting aside judgment rendered by Court of Session - Hence, present appeal - Whether order of alteration of forum for trial was justified.

Brief Facts:

Complaints were filed against the private parties, for offences punishable under the Securities and Exchange Board of India Act, 1992 . The change of 'forum' for trial, was assailed by some of the private parties, before the Court to which the matters were committed. Their challenge failed. The matters were then carried, to the High Court. Alternatively, some of the private parties, directly approached the jurisdictional High Court, to assail the changed 'forum' of trial. A Division Bench of the High Court, through the impugned judgment collectively disposed of all matters pending before it, by setting aside the judgment rendered by the Court of Session. The SEBI therefore approached this Court to assail the judgment rendered by the High Court.

Held while allowing the petition:

(i) Section 26(2) of the Act expressly provided, No court inferior to that of a Metropolitan Magistrate (or, a Judicial Magistrate of the first class) shall try an offence punishable under this Act. It was therefore apparent, that it was not imperative, that the forum for trial of offences under the unamended Section 24 of the Act would be conducted only by a Metropolitan Magistrate (or, a Judicial Magistrate of the first class). Trials for offences under the SEBI Act, even prior to the Amendment Act, could well have been conducted by a Court of Session, or an Additional Sessions Judge. [51]

(ii) The forum for trial earlier vested in the Court of Metropolitan Magistrate or, Judicial Magistrate of the first class was retrospectively amended, inasmuch as, the forum of trial after the Amendment Act was retrospectively changed to the Court of Session. The trials even in respect of offences allegedly committed before the date Amendment Act became operational, whether in respect whereof trial had or had not been initiated, would stand jurisdictionally vested in a Court of Session. And likewise, trials of offences under the SEBI Act, consequent upon 'the Amendment Act would stand jurisdictionally transferred for trial to a Special Court, irrespective of whether the offence under the SEBI Act was committed before the date Amendment Act became operational, and irrespective of the fact whether trial had or had not been initiated. [56].

VIII

Chintalapati Srinivasa Raju and Ors. Vs. Securities and Exchange Board of India, 2018

Relevant Sections:

Securities and Exchange Board of India Regulation2(c), Regulation 2(e)

Equivalent Citation:

AIR2018SC2411, IV(2018)BC617(SC), 2018 (3) CCC 26 , [2018]145CLA150(SC), [2018]210CompCas285(SC), (2018)4CompLJ17(SC), (2018)5MLJ857, 2018(7)SCALE721, (2018)7SCC443, [2018]148SCL1(SC), MANU/SC/0598/2018

Case Note:

Capital Market - Securities market - Restriction to access - Appellant, who was executive director was confined to operating a joint venture company of - Company declared bonus, thereby doubling number of shares held by Appellant and consequently, shareholding of Appellant increased - By show cause notice, it was stated that as Appellant was promoter and director of company, he was liable as insider, having knowledge of UPSI, as result of which he stood to gain by selling shares which he owned at inflated value - Whole Time Member of SEBI held that fact that books of accounts of company were fabricated and manipulated remains within knowledge and possession of insiders who were reasonably expected to have access to them - It was then held that Appellant was barred from accessing securities market for period of seven years and further, Appellant was to disgorge amount mentioned against his name - Appeal to Appellate Tribunal was largely dismissed by majority judgment - Majority judgment held that since there was no real difference between a executive and a non-executive director, he would reasonably be expected to know about fraud and manipulation by Chairman and his cohorts - Hence, present appeal - Whether Appellant was in any manner responsible for actions taken by management of company and had any role in fraud committed by company.

Brief Facts:

The Appellant, who was an executive director of company was confined to operating a joint venture company. The company declared a bonus, thereby doubling the number of shares held by the Appellant. Consequently, the shareholding of the Appellant increased. By a show cause notice, it was stated that as the Appellant was a promoter and director of company, he was liable as an insider, having knowledge of UPSI, as a result of which he stood to gain by selling shares which he owned at an inflated value. After referring to Regulations 2(c) and 2(e) of the 1992 Regulations, the Whole Time Member held that being a director of company, the Appellant was a connected person under Regulation 2(c) and, therefore, an insider under Regulation 2(e). The Whole Time Member went on to hold that the fact that the books of accounts of company were fabricated and manipulated remains within the knowledge and possession of insiders who were reasonably expected to have access to them. It was then held that the Appellant was barred from accessing the securities market for a period of seven years. Further, the Appellant was to disgorge the amount mentioned against his name. An appeal to the Appellate Tribunal was largely dismissed by the majority judgment. The majority judgment held that since there was no real difference between an executive and a non-executive director, he would reasonably be expected to know about the fraud and manipulation by the Chairman and his cohorts, as he was closely connected to the same, being his co-brother. It was held by the majority judgment of the Appellate Tribunal that the Appellant being a promoter was not the only ground of violation of the 1992 Regulations, but being a director of company and co-brother of shareholder would also rope the Appellant in. However, the Appellant was given relief to the extent that under the Explanation to Regulation 2(e) of the 1992 Regulations, the Appellant could only be held liable for a period of six months beyond his resignation as a director. A remand order, therefore, was made to assess the quantum of unlawful gains that the Appellant had made.

Held, while allowing the appeal:

The Appellant attended only six out of ten board meetings of company for the period that he was a non-executive director. The Appellant was not involved in any business development, diversification plans and advise on new ventures of company. It was also held by the minority judgment that the findings of the Whole Time Member and the majority went clearly beyond the show cause notice, makes it clear that the Appellant is only sought to be roped in as a promoter. Once it was found that he was not a promoter, then the basis of the show cause notice goes as also the basis of the impugned judgment. [18]

(iii) The Appellant attended only six out of ten board meetings of company for the period that he was a non-executive director. The Appellant was not involved in any business development, diversification plans and advise on new ventures of company. It was also held by the minority judgment that the findings of the Whole Time Member and the majority went clearly beyond the show cause notice, makes it clear that the Appellant is only sought to be roped in as a promoter. Once it was found that he was not a promoter, then the basis of the show cause notice goes as also the basis of the impugned judgment.

IX

Securities and Exchange Board of India vs Udayant Malhotra, 2020

Relevant Section:

Securities And Exchange Board Of India Act, 1992 - Section 11(4)

Equivalent Citation:

(2021)1SCC219, [2021]164SCL75(SC), MANU/SC/0894/2020

Case Notes:

Capital Market-Selling of Shares - Notional gain allegedly made - Investigation - Ex-parte order passed during pandemic - Sustainability thereof in investigation pending for three years - Respondent, CEO and MD of Company alleged of selling shares with inside price knowledge - Investigation in process for three years - Ex-parte orders passed during pandemic - Tribunal set aside the order vide impugned finding - Whether any ex-parte order could have been passed during pandemic in the absence of any extreme urgency?

Brief Facts:

The Respondent, Chief Executive Officer and Managing Director of the Company in o?=question was alleged of sellingshares o?=of the Company having inside knowledge of price sensitive information, namely, the unaudited financial results for the relevant o?=quarter. It was alleged that the financial results were approved by the Board of Directors, upon which the price of the scrips of the Company sustained a drastic reduction. Respondent was alleged to have made notional gain or averted a notional loss. The sales made by the Respondent was subjected to investigation. The Whole Time Member passed an ex parte order against Respondent. Respondent in appeal questioned the passing of ex-parte order during the pandemic. Impugned order held that there was no extreme urgency pass an ex-parte interim order without considering the balance of convenience or irreparable injury. Hence, the present Appeal.

Held, while disposing the Appeal:

Tribunalwas correct in coming to the conclusion that since the investigation was pending since 2017 and information had been supplied on 28 November 2019, there was no urgency for passing an ex-parte interim order of the nature that was issued by the Whole Time Member. [5]

The observations made in impugned order about power of SEBI clarified as not to be cited as precedent o?=in any other case. The order passed by the SEBI must necessarily be in accord with Section 11(4) of the SEBI Act.

Appeals disposed of.

X

Adjudicating Officer Securities and Exchange Board of India Vs. Bhavesh Pabari, 2019

Relevant Sections:

Securities And Exchange Board Of India Act, 1992 - Section 15-J; Securities And Exchange Board Of India Act, 1992 - Section 15-A; Securities And Exchange Board Of India Act, 1992 - Section 15-HA

Equivalent Citation: AIR2019SC1265, II(2019)BC1(SC), [2019]149CLA311(SC), [2019]213CompCas439(SC), (2019)3CompLJ1(SC), 2019(4)SCALE58, (2019)5SCC90, 2019 (5) SCJ 416, [2019]152SCL717(SC), MANU/SC/0296/2019

Case Notes:

Capital Market - Quantum of penalty - Section 15-J of Securities and Exchange Board of India Act, 1992 ("SEBI Act") - Issue in present case was relating to determining quantum of penalty imposable by Adjudicating Authority - Whether conditions stipulated in Clauses (a), (b) and (c) of Section 15-J of ("SEBI Act") were exhaustive to govern discretion in Adjudicating Officer to decide on quantum of penalty or said conditions were merely illustrative - Whether power and discretion vested by Section 15-J of SEBI Act to decide on quantum of penalty, regardless of manner in which first question is answered, stands eclipsed by penalty provisions contained in Section 15-A to Section 15-HA of SEBI Act.

Brief Facts:

Issue in present case was relating to determining quantum of penalty imposable by Adjudicating Authority. Question raised is whether conditions stipulated in Clauses (a), (b) and (c) of Section 15-J of ("SEBI Act") were exhaustive to govern discretion in Adjudicating Officer to decide on quantum of penalty or said conditions were merely illustrative. Held, while disposing of the appeal 1. A narrow view would be in direct conflict with the provisions of Section 15-I(2) of the SEBI Act which vests jurisdiction in the Adjudicating Officer, who is empowered on completion of the inquiry to impose "such penalty as he thinks fit in accordance with the provisions of any of those sections."[9] 2. The circumstances enumerated in Clauses (a), (b) and (c) of Section 15-J of the SEBI Act may have no relevance and may never arise in case of contraventions contemplated by certain provisions of the SEBI Act, for instance Section 15-A, 15-B or 15-C of the SEBI Act. Failure to furnish information, return, etc.; failure to enter into agreement with clients; and failure to redress investors' grievances cannot give rise to the circumstances set out in Clauses (a), (b) and (c) of Section 15-J.[10]

Held while disposing off the appeal,

C.A. No. 9798/2014 preferred by M/s. Shree Radhe and C.A. No. 9797/ 2014 preferred by Bhavesh Pabari hold no merit and are dismissed affirming the order passed by the Appellate Tribunal and confirming the penalty of Rs. 20,00,000 each imposed under Section 15-HA of the Act.[20] 9. The reference made vide order dated 14th March, 2016 and the above captioned Civil Appeals are, accordingly, disposed of. In the facts and circumstances of the cases, there shall be no order as to costs.[52]

XI

Videocon International ltd Vs. Securities and Exchange Board of India, 2015

Relevant Section:

SECURITIES AND EXCHANGE BOARD OF INDIA ACT, 1992 - Section 15Z; SECURITIES AND EXCHANGE BOARD OF INDIA ACT, 1992 - Section 15Y

Equivalent Citation: 2015(2)ABR206, 2015II AD (S.C.) 351, AIR2015SC1042, 1(2015)BC443(SC), 2015 (3) CCC 260 , [2015]124CLA289(SC), 119(2015)CLT799(SC), [2015]188CompCas566(SC), (2015)1CompLJ465(SC), 2015-5-LW551, 2015(1)SCALE293, (2015)4SCC33, 2015 (4) SCJ 566, [2015]129SCL673(SC), MANU/SC/0023/2015

Case notes:

SEBI- Maintainability of appeal - Pre-amendment - Section 15Z of Securities and Exchange Board of India Act, 1992 and Section 6 of General Clauses Act, 1897 - High Court held that appeals as had been filed before coming into force of amended Section 15Z of Act, would not be affected by amendment, and High Court had jurisdiction to hear and dispose of same - Hence, present appeal - Whether appeals preferred by Respondent before amendment was maintainable - Held, Appellate remedy available to Respondent prior to amendment of Section 15Z of SEBI Act, must continue to be available to Respondent, despite amendment - Appellant was not justified in contending that instant amendment to Section 15Z of SEBI Act, did not affect second appellate remedy, but merely alters forum where second appellate remedy would lie, was not acceptable - Since all such appeals as had been filed by Board, prior before amendment of Section 15Z, would have to be accepted as vested, and must be adjudicated accordingly - Conclusion emerges even from mandate contained in Section 6 of General Clauses Act, 1897 - All appeals preferred by Respondent, before High Court, were maintainable - [paras 32, 33 and 34]

Held while dismissing the appeal,

we find no merit in this appeal and the same is accordingly dismissed. It is, however, necessary for us to record, that the impugned order was passed with reference to a number of appeals, which were preferred by the Board, as against a common order passed by the Securities Appellate Tribunal. In the impugned order, some of the appeals preferred by the Board were held as maintainable before the High Court, whilst a different view was expressed with reference to the appeals preferred by the Board after 29.10.2002. We have concluded, that all appeals preferred by the Respondent herein, before the High Court, were maintainable. In exercise of our jurisdiction Under Article 142 of the Constitution of India, we direct, that the instant order passed by us would govern all cases which were disposed of by the High Court through the impugned order dated 13.10.2003.

35. Disposed of accordingly.

XII

Ritesh Agarwal and Ors. Vs securities and Exchange Board of India and Ors., 2009

Relevant Section:

SECURITIES AND EXCHANGE BOARD OF INDIA ACT, 1992 - Section 15Z; SECURITIES AND EXCHANGE BOARD OF INDIA ACT, 1992 - Section 15Y

Equivalent Citation: 2009(5)ALT14(SC), I(2010)BC550, I(2010)BC550(SC), [2008]85CLA35(SC), 3(2008)CLT871, [2008]144CompCas12(SC), (2008)5CompLJ119(SC), JT2008(7)SC289, 2008(9)SCALE29, (2008)8SCC205, [2008]84SCL373(SC), MANU/SC/2178/2009

Case Notes:

Company-Fraud - Appellants, for committed fraud on public as well as company board debarred from having access to capital market for a period of 10 years and directed to buy back their shares - Appeal - Appellants contended that two of the appellants were minor, thus, could not be punished - Further, contended that appellants were not the promoters of the company and could not be held liable - Held, as established that two of the appellants were minor, they could not entered into contract and not held liable - However, other appellants who were made mis-representation and committed fraud would be penalised for the same - Also established that appellants were promoters of the company - Appeal allowed to the extent that direction of board not applicable to minor appellants

Ratio Decidendi:"*Appellants who were made mis-representation and committed fraud would be penalised for the same*"

Held while allowing the appeal,

We, however, uphold other directions issued by the Board including the action taken in respect of the offences purported to have been committed. We also grant liberty to the authorities to proceed against the offenders not only for other or further charges to which they made themselves liable under the SEBI Act but also under the Companies Act, 1956 and other penal statutes, if attracted.

17. For the reasons aforementioned, the appeal is allowed to the aforementioned extent. No costs.

XIII

Prakash Gupta vs Securities and Exchange Board of India, 2021

Relevant Section:

Securities And Exchange Board Of India Act, 1992 - Section 24A

Equivalent Citation: AIR2021SC3601, 2021 (2) ALT (Crl.) 441 (A.P.), IV(2021)BC1(SC), 2021(4)BLJ439, 2021(3)MLJ(Crl)387, 2021(3)RCR(Criminal)585, [2021]167SCL560(SC), MANU/SC/0469/2021

Case Notes:

Capital Market - Compounding of offence - Contravention of Statutory Provisions - Prosecution under Section 24(1) of the Securities and Exchange Board of India Act, 1992 (SEBI Act) - Application seeking compounding rejected - Objection of the Securities and Exchange Board of India that offence could not be compounded without its consent upheld - High Court affirmed Order of the Trial Court - Hence, the present appeal - Whether application seeking compounding rightly rejected?

Brief Facts:

Appellant, director and promoter of a company incorporated initially as a private limited company. Subsequently its status changed to that of a public limited company. It then made an Initial Public Offer (IPO) inviting a subscription to 38 lac equity shares at a par value of Rs. 10 per share. SEBI received a complaint that certain Delhi/Bombay based brokers had, on the instructions of the Company, purchased its shares and that huge deliveries were kept outstanding in the grey market. SEBI also received an anonymous complaint alleging price rigging and insider trading in the scrip of the Company. After a preliminary inquiry SEBI initiated an investigation. SEBI came up with the name of six entities who had purchased approximately 51 per cent of the 38 lac equity shares on offer. They were found to have continued buying shares even after that period, and had ultimately purchased 28,38,000 equity shares, which was approximately 75 per cent of the post issue floating stock of the Company. As such, it was assumed that these entities were, therefore, responsible for the upward price movement in the scrip.When SEBI issued summons to these six entities, it was the Appellant who replied to them. In a statement given to SEBI Appellant admitted that these entities were directly/ indirectly related to the Company and its directors, and that he managed their day-to-day affairs. SEBI filed a criminal complaint alleging violations of Regulations 4(a) and 4(e) of the 1995 PFUTP Regulations, read with Regulations 6(1), 6(3), 8(1), 10(1) and 10(2) of the 1994 Takeover Regulations, which are punishable under Sections 24 and 27 of the SEBI Act followed by further actions. Appellant together with the other Accused instituted proceedings under Section 482 of the Code of Criminal Procedure, 1973 for quashing the complaint case and summoning order. The proceedings remained pending for about six years, until they were eventually dismissed. Appellant and the other Accused persons filed a 'consent application' with SEBI, which was returned with the intimation that the Appellant and other Accused persons could file an appropriate application for compounding in the criminal case. Application was filed and SEBI referred the same to seek views of its High Powered Advisory Committee (HPAC) which advised against compounding. Application was dismissed. A revision petition filed to challenge the dismissal also dismissed by Single Judge of the High Court.

Held, while dismissing the Appeal:

Section 24A does not stipulate that the consent of SEBI is necessary for the SAT or the Court before which such proceedings are pending to compound an offence.[84]

Section 24(1) is an omnibus provision for all offences punishable for contravention (or attempts or abetments) of the provisions of the Act or of any Rule or Regulation made under it. Offences punishable under Sub-section (1) of Section 24 would cover a range of violations from the venial to the serious. The entrustment of the power to compound offences either before or after the institution of any proceeding is to SAT or a Court before which such proceedings are pending. The provisions of Section 24A must be read in a manner consistent with the object and purpose underlying the position of SEBI as an expert regulator. [89]

While the statute has entrusted the powers of compounding offences to SAT or to the Court, as the case may be, before which the proceedings are pending, the view of SEBI as an expert regulator must necessarily be borne in mind by the SAT and the Court, and would be entitled to a degree of deference. While SEBI does not have a veto, having regard to the language of Section 24A, its views must be elicited. The Court must be wary of substituting its own wisdom on the gravity of the offence or the impact on the markets, while discarding the expert opinion of the SEBI.[90]

Legislative scheme of the SEBI Act delineates several actions that are liable for penalty under Section 15, but includes a common sentencing provision under Section 24. Therefore, Section 24 would be the sentencing provision for the most banal of offences, to the most egregious of market disruptions and frauds. [91]

In the present case, the nature of the allegations against the Appellant are such so as to preclude a decision to compound the offences. Allegations in the present case involved serious acts which impinged upon the protection of investors and the stability of the securities' market. SEBI was justified in opposing the request for the compounding of the offences. The matter was referred to the HPAC constituted by SEBI and presided over by a former judge of the Bombay High Court, which denied the request for compounding. This decision which has been taken by SEBI is not mala fide nor does it suffer from manifest arbitrariness.

XIV

Securities and Exchange Board Vs. Rakhi Trading Private Limited, 2018

Relevant Section:

SECURITIES AND EXCHANGE BOARD OF INDIA ACT, 1992 - Section 15Z; SECURITIES AND EXCHANGE BOARD OF INDIA ACT, 1992 - Section 15Y

Equivalent Citation: 2018 2 AWC1989SC, III(2018)BC302(SC), 2018(3)BomCR192, [2018]143CLA15(SC), [2018]207CompCas443(SC), (2018)2CompLJ1(SC), 2018(2)SCALE156, (2018)13SCC753, [2018]146SCL163(SC), MANU/SC/0096/2018

Case Notes:

SEBI - Fraudulent trade - Imposition of penalty - Regulations 3(a), 3(b), 3(c) and 4(1), 4(2)(a) and 4(2)(b) of Securities and Exchange Board of India Regulations, 2003, Regulations 7A(1), 7A(2), 7A(3) and 7A(4) of Securities and Exchange Board of India Regulations, 1992 and Section 15HA and 15T of Securities and Exchange Board of India Act, 1992 - Show cause notice issued against Respondents alleging that parties were buying and selling securities in derivatives segment at price which did not reflect value of underlying in synchronised and reverse transactions - SEBI proceeded against traders for violation of Regulations 3(a), (b) and (c) and 4(1), (2)(a) and (b) of Securities and Exchange Board of India Regulations, 2003 - In case of brokers, charge was that they also violated Regulations 7A(1), (2), (3) and (4) of Regulations, 1992 - Penalty was imposed under Section 15HA of Act - Appeal was filed under Section 15T before SAT - Securities Appellate Tribunal (SAT) set aside decisions of A.O - Hence, present appeal - Whether Respondents were engaged in fraudulent trade and liable for imposition of penalty.

Brief Facts:

The show cause notices issued against Appellants alleging that the parties were buying and selling securities in the derivatives segment at a price which did not reflect the value of the underlying in synchronised and reverse transactions. According to the A.O. a manipulative/deceptive devise was used for synchronization of trades and the trades were fraudulent/ fictitious in nature. It was found that there was violation of Regulations 3(a), (b) and (c) and 4(1), (2)(a) and (b) of the PFUTP Regulations, 2003. Consequently, a penalty was imposed under Section 15HA of the SEBI Act, 1992. Appeal was filed under Section 15T before the SAT. An appeal was disposed of whereby SAT set aside the order of SEBI.

Held, while disposing off the appeal:

Considering the reversal transactions, quantity, price and time and sale, parties being persistent in number of such trade transactions with huge price variations, it would be too naive to hold that the transactions were through screen-based trading and hence anonymous. Such conclusion would be over-looking the prior meeting of minds involving synchronization of buy and sell order and not negotiated deals as per the board's circular. The impugned transactions were manipulative/deceptive device to create a desired loss and/or profit. Such synchronized trading was violative of transparent norms of trading in securities. If the findings of SAT were to be sustained, it would have serious repercussions undermining the integrity of the market and the impugned order of SAT was liable to be set aside.

XV

Securities and Exchange Board of India and Ors. vs. Kanaiyalal Baldevbhai Patel and Ors.

Relevant sections:

Securities and Exchange Board of India Act, 1992 - Section 12, Securities and Exchange Board of India Act, 1992 - Section 12A, Securities and Exchange Board of India Act, 1992 - Section 15HA, Securities and Exchange Board of India Act, 1992 - Section 30; Indian Contract Act, 1872; Monopolies and Restrictive Trade Practices Act, 1969 [Repealed] - Section 36A; Consumer Protection Act, 1986 - Section 2(1); Competition Act, 2002 - Section 3; Food Safety and Standards Act, 2006 - Section 24(2); Specific Relief Act 1963 - Section 20; Usurious Loans Act, 1918 - Section 3; Securities and Exchange Board of India (Prohibition of Fraudulent and Unfair Trade Practices relating to Securities Market) Regulations, 1995

Equivalent Citation: IV(2017)BC643(SC), [2017]141CLA254(SC), [2018]207CompCas416(SC), (2017)4CompLJ401(SC), 2017(4)RCR(Civil)660, 2017(11)SCALE600, (2017)15SCC1, 2017 (8) SCJ 650, [2017]144SCL5(SC), MANU/SC/1188/2017

Case Notes:

Capital Market - Imposition of penalty - Prohibition of Fraudulent and Unfair Trade Practices relating to Securities Market) Regulations, 2003 - Adjudicating Authorities imposed penalty on Respondents - Securities Appellate Tribunal before whom appeals were filed by Respondents interfered with orders passed by Adjudicating Authority primarily on ground that on reading of Regulation 2(c),(3) and Regulation (4) of Regulations it did not transpire that acts attributable amount to fraudulent or unfair trade practice warranting findings recorded by Adjudicating Authority and imposition of penalty in question on that basis - Hence, present appeal - Whether front running by non-intermediary was prohibited practice under Regulations 3 (a), (b), (c) and (d) and 4(1) of Regulations.

Brief Facts:

The Securities Appellate Tribunal before whom appeals were filed by the Respondents interfered with the orders passed by the Adjudicating Authority primarily on the ground that on a reading of Regulation 2(c),(3) and Regulation (4) of the Regulations it did not transpire that the acts attributable amount to fraudulent or unfair trade practice warranting the findings recorded by the Adjudicating Authority and the imposition of penalty in question on that basis. Hence, present appeal.

Held, while allowing the appeal:

(i) The law of confidentiality had a bearing on this case instant. Confidential information acquired or compiled by a corporation in the course and conduct of its business was a species of property to which the corporation has the exclusive right and benefit, and which a Court of equity will protect through the injunctive process or other appropriate remedy. The information of possible trades that the company was going to undertake is the confidential information of the company concerned, which it has absolute liberty to deal with. Therefore, a person conveying confidential information to another person (tippee) breaches his duty prescribed by law and if the recipient of such information knows of the breach and trades, and there was an inducement to bring about an inequitable result, then the recipient tippee may be said to have committed the fraud. [42]

(ii) Accordingly, non-intermediary front running may be brought under the prohibition prescribed under Regulations 3 and 4 (1), for being fraudulent or unfair trade practice, provided that the ingredients under those heads were satisfied. It was clear that in order to establish charges against tippee, Under Regulations 3 (a), (b), (c) and (d) and 4 (1) of FUTP 2003, one needs to prove that a person who had provided the tip was under a duty to keep the non-public information under confidence, further such breach of duty was known to the tippee and he still trades thereby defrauding the person, whose orders were front-runned, by inducing him to deal at the price he did. [43] Ranjan Gogoi, J.: Concurring view

(iii) To attract the rigor of Regulations 3 and 4 of the 2003 Regulations, mens rea was not an indispensable requirement and the correct test is one of preponderance of probabilities. Merely because the operation of the aforesaid two provisions of the 2003 Regulations invite penal consequences on the defaulters, proof beyond reasonable doubt as held by present Court in Securities and Exchange Board of India v. Kishore R. Ajmera was not an indispensable requirement. The inferential conclusion from the proved and admitted facts, so long the same were reasonable and could be legitimately arrived at on a consideration of the totality of the materials, would be permissible and legally justified. Having regard to the facts of the present cases i.e. the volume of shares sold and purchased; the proximity of time between the transactions of sale and purchase and the repeated nature of transactions on different dates, the conduct of the Respondents were in breach of the code of business integrity in the securities market. The consequences for such breach including penal consequences. Orders passed by the Appellate Tribunal were set aside and the findings recorded and the penalty imposed by the Adjudicating Officer were restored. [58]

XVI

Franklinn Templeton Trustee Services Private ltd and Ors Vs. Amruta Garg and Ors., 2021

Relevant Sections: Securities and Exchange Board (Intermediaries) Regulations, 2008; Securities and Exchange Board (Mutual Funds) (Amendment) Regulations, 2021;; Securities And Exchange Board Of India Act, 1992 - Section 11, Securities And Exchange Board Of India Act, 1992 Section 12, Securities And Exchange Board Of India Act, 1992 - Section 15A

Equivalent Citation: IV(2017)BC643(SC), [2017]141CLA254(SC), [2018]207CompCas416(SC), (2017)4CompLJ401(SC), 2017(4)RCR(Civil)660, 2017(11)SCALE600, (2017)15SCC1, 2017 (8) SCJ 650, [2017]144SCL5(SC), MANU/SC/1188/2021

Case Note:

Capital Market - Winding up of Mutual Fund Schemes - Scope of Judicial Review - Interpretation of Regulation 18(15)(c) of the Securities and Exchange Board of India (Mutual Funds) Regulations, 1996 (Regulations) - Binding effect of Winding Up of Schemes - Determination thereof - Whether consent in respect of winding up applicable to all unit holders or to those who gave consent?

Brief Facts:

The present matter came up to interpret Regulation 18(15)(c) of the Securities and Exchange Board of India (Mutual Funds) Regulations, 1996 and accepting the poll results in respect of winding up of six mutual fund schemes. The interpretation also to be made in regard to interrelation of Regulations 39 to 42 and examining challenge to the constitutional validity of Regulations 39 to 42.

Held, while disposing the Appeal:

The distinction between Regulation 18(15A) and Regulation 18(15)(c) is evident. The words 'winding up or premature redemption of units' in Regulation 18(15)(c) refers to a situation covered by Regulation 39(2)(a), that is, when the scheme is being wound up pursuant to a decision of the trustees. On the other hand, Regulation 18(15A) does not apply when the scheme is being wound up, rather it applies when there is a proposal to change the fundamental attributes of the scheme, fee or expense or any other change that would modify the scheme and affect the interests of the unitholders. The effect should be not to wind up the scheme thereby bringing it to an end, but to continue with the scheme as modified. Therefore, for Regulation 18(15A) to apply, the scheme should not cease to exist.[33]

'Consent' for the purpose of Regulation 18(15)(c) refers to the consent of the majority of the unitholders present and voting, and in case of a poll, the computation would be with reference to the number of units held by the unitholder. In fact, in the course of hearing, it was conceded that majority of the unitholders belong to provident fund trusts or pension funds. The voting pattern referred to in our earlier order reflects that voting Under Regulation 18(15)(c) is possible and can work smoothly without much difficulty. The apprehensions expressed, therefore, do not carry much weight. It is obvious that where the unitholders vote against winding up, consequences would follow and accordingly the scheme would not be wound up. This is a natural and normal consequence which will have to be given effect to. It would, as stated above, happen rarely and that too would not happen without any genuine and good reason.[37]

The language of Clauses (a) and (c) to sub-Regulation (2), and sub-Regulation (3) to Regulation 39 does not envisage involvement of the unitholders till the publication of notices in case of Clauses (b) and (c) to sub-Regulation (2) to Regulation 39. Therefore, when Clauses (a) or (c) of Regulation 39(2) apply, the unitholders are to be informed about the winding up by the trustees or SEBI by way of public notice. Publication in terms of Regulation 39(3) is even required when the unitholders vote for winding up of a scheme under Clause (b) of Regulation 39(2).[40]

To complete interpretation of Regulation 18(15), it is to state that Clause (a) applies and requires the trustees to obtain consent of the unitholders whenever required by SEBI in the interest of the unitholders. Clause (b) states that the trustees would obtain consent of the unitholders whenever required to do so on the requisition made by three-fourths of the unitholders of any scheme. Accordingly, Clause (a) would apply whenever SEBI mandates and Clause (b) applies whenever three-fourths of the unitholders of the scheme make a requisition.[45]

The Regulations rightly draw the distinction between creditors and the unitholders. The unit holders are investors who take the risk and, therefore, entitled to profits and gains. Having taken the calculated risk, they must also bear the losses, if any. Unitholders are not entitled to fixed return or even protection of the principal amount. Creditors, on the other hand, are entitled to fixed return as per mutually agreed contracts. Their rate of return is in the nature of interest and not profit or loss. Creditors are not risk takers as is the case with the unitholders. In this sense, unitholders are somewhat at par with the shareholders of a company.[61]

Since the Regulations are in the nature of economic Regulations, while exercising the power of judicial review, restraint to be exercised unless clear grounds justify interference. Policy decisions can only be faulted on the grounds of mala fides, unreasonableness, arbitrariness and unfairness, in addition to violation of fundamental rights or exercise of power beyond the legal limits. The principle of manifest arbitrariness requires something to be done in exercise in the form of delegated legislation which is capricious, irrational or without adequate determining principle. Delegated legislations that are forbiddingly excessive or disproportionate can also be manifestly arbitrary. Regulations under challenge does not suffer from the vice of manifest arbitrariness.[63]

Legal interpretation of Regulation 18(15)(c) and Regulations 39 to 42 to the extent indicated above are conclusive and binding. For clarity, we would also observe that any finding given by the High Court on facts or even on legal issues not subject matter of this Order or our earlier Order dated 12th February, 2021 would not be treated as conclusive and binding as the findings are sub-judice and pending before this Court on interpretation as well as merits.[68]

XVII

The Chairman, SEBI vs. Shriram Mutual Funds and Ors., 2006

Relevant Section:

SECURITIES AND EXCHANGE BOARD OF INDIA ACT, 1992 - Section 15 D (b); SECURITIES AND EXCHANGE BOARD OF INDIA ACT, 1992 - Section 15 E

Citations: MANU/SC/8185/2006

Case Note:

Company - penalty - Regulation 15 (D)(b) of the Securities and Exchange Board of India Act, 1992 - respondent was mutual fund - floated five schemes - failed to comply with terms and conditions attached to Certificate of Registration which were statutory in nature as prescribed by Regulation 15 (D)(b) - whether once it is conclusively established that mutual fund had violated terms of Certificate of Registration and the statutory Regulations imposition of penalty becomes a sine qua non of violation - respondent aware that they were acting in violation of provisions of regulations - penalty is attracted as soon as contravention of statutory obligation as contemplated by Act and Regulation was established and hence intention of parties committing such violation becomes wholly irrelevant.

Held,

In our view, the impugned judgment of the Securities appellate Tribunal has set a serious wrong precedent and the powers of the SEBI to impose penalty under Chapter VIA are severely curtailed against the plain language of the statute which mandatorily imposes penalties on the contravention of the Act/Regulations without any requirement of the contravention having been deliberated or contumacious. The impugned order sets the stage for various market players to violate statutory regulations with impunity and subsequently plead ignorance of law or lack of mens rea to escape the imposition of penalty. The imputing mens rea into the provisions of Chapter VI A is against the plain language of the statute and frustrates entire purpose and object of introducing Chapter VIA to give teeth to the SEBI to secure strict compliance of the Act and the Regulations.

22. In the result, the Civil Appeal Nos. 9523 and 9524 of 2003 are allowed and the order passed by the Securities Appellate Tribunal, Mumbai dated 21.08.2003 in Appeal Nos. 50 and 51 of 2002 are set aside. No costs.

XVIII

Securities and Exchange Board of India vs Opee Stock link and Ors., 2016

Relevant Section:

SECURITIES AND EXCHANGE BOARD OF INDIA ACT, 1992 - Section 12A(a); SECURITIES AND EXCHANGE BOARD OF INDIA ACT, 1992 - Section 12(b); SECURITIES AND EXCHANGE BOARD OF INDIA ACT, 1992 - Section 12(c)

Equivalent Citations:

AIR2016SC3825, 2016(4)ALLMR979, III(2016)BC694(SC), [2016]133CLA251(SC), [2016]197CompCas435(SC), 120(2)CWN94, 2016(4)RCR(Civil)43, 2016(6)SCALE716, (2016)14SCC134, [2016]137SCL24(SC), MANU/SC/0755/2016

Case Note:

SEBI - Violation of provision - Imposition of Penalty - Section 12A(a), (b), (c) of Securities and Exchange Board of India Act, 1992 (Act); Section 2(i)(b) of Securities Contracts (Regulation) Act, 1956 (SCRA) - Appeals were filed against order passed by Tribunal, whereby Tribunal allowed appeals filed by Respondents and set aside orders passed by Whole Time Member and Adjudicating Officer - Whether Whole Time Member and Adjudicating Officer were justified in imposing penalty upon Respondents for violation of provisions of Section 12A(a), (b), (c) of Act

Brief Facts:

When shares of Jet Airways Limited and Infrastructure Development Finance Company Limited were offered to public at large, the issue of shares in relation to both companies had been over subscribed. It was brought to notice of Security and Exchange Board of India (SEBI) that several serious irregularities/illegalities had been committed by some persons. In investigations made by officials of SEBI, it was revealed that in matter of IPO of afore stated companies, shares which were meant for RIIs had been cornered through hundreds of benami/fictitious demat account holders, which was in violation of provisions of Section 12A (a), (b), (c) of Act. Moreover, it was also found that said transactions were in violation of Regulations 3 and 4(1) of Securities and Exchange Board of India (Prohibition of Fraudulent and Unfair Trade Practices Relating to Securities Markets) Regulations, 2003 (Regulations). Upon knowing nature of transactions, Whole Time Member of SEBI was convinced that all transactions pertaining to opening of demat accounts, applications made by applicants holding demat accounts, sale by those account holders to Respondents and sale by Respondents to other buyers of shares were of fishy nature. There is a specific finding by Whole Time Member of SEBI, who has thoroughly examined facts of case and has come to conclusion, like a trial court, to the effect that demat accounts were signed by some persons with different spellings of their names and in different manners.

Held, while disposing off the Appeals:

1. Most of demat account holders were not having their trading accounts and many of them were having a common address. Normally, a demat account holder, if a genuine one, would use his own correct address while opening and operating his demat account. Number of demat account were having same address and that too, care of someone else and this makes genuineness of account holders and transactions doubtful.[10]

2. From all transactions, which were in nature of a scam, it was clear that demat account holders were not genuine and either they were benami or fictitious and shares were purchased on behalf of someone, who had financed these demat account holders and a show was made as if shares were finally sold to concerned Respondents. Entire chain of transactions of shares and doubtful nature of demat holders, established the fact that all these transactions were nothing but a scam.[11]

3. Whole Time Member of SEBI had very meticulously examined all facts and rightly concluded that dealings of Respondents were not fair and were in violation of Act as well as Regulations.[13]

10. Appeals filed by SEBI were allowed and orders passed by Tribunal were quashed so as to give effect to orders passed by Whole Time Member as well as Adjudicating Officer, SEBI.[25]

XIX

Arun Kumar Agrawal Vs. Union of India and Ors., 2013

Relevant Section:

Securities and Exchange Board of India Act, 1992 - Section 4(5)

Equivalent Citation: 2013XII AD (S.C.) 157, 2014 (4) AWC 3405 (SC), 2013(6)BomCR530, (2014)1CompLJ39(SC), 2013(5)ESC820(SC), 2013(4)ESC696(SC), JT2013(14)SC563, (2013)8MLJ332, 2013(13)SCALE442, (2014)2SCC609, (2014)1SCC(LS)433, 2014 (1) SCJ 231, [2013]3SCR508, 2014(1)SCT617(SC), 2014(4)SLR313(SC), MANU/SC/1146/2013

Case Notes: Constitution of India - Article 32--Writ of quo warranto--Employment--Removal--Writ petition seeks issuance of writ of quo warranto or any other direction against Chairman of Securities and Exchange Board of India (S.E.B.I.) and his consequential removal from post of Chairman--Petitioner stool pigeon acting on directions of business houses--Anxiety of business houses for removal of Chairman of S.E.B.I.--Not wholly unimaginable--Appointment to such high powered position actually made fairly and in accordance with procedure established by law--Writ petition lacks merit and dismissed.

Brief Facts:

This writ petition has been filed by one Mr. Arun Kumar Agrawal under Article 32 of the Constitution of India; seeks the issuance of a writ of quo warranto or any other direction against Mr. U.K. Sinha, Chairman of the

Securities and Exchange Board of India (hereinafter referred to as 'SEBI') and his consequential removal from the post of Chairman.

2. Stated concisely, the Petitioner challenges the appointment of Respondent No. 4 on the following grounds:

(a) Mr. Sinha failed to fulfill one of the eligibility condition as laid down in Sub-section (5) of Section 4 of the Securities and Exchange Board of India Act, 1992 (hereinafter referred to as 'SEBI Act'), as well as the qualification contained in Government communication, which required that the Chairman shall be a person of high integrity.

(b) The appointment of Respondent No. 4 is the result of manipulation, misrepresentation and suppression of vital material before the Search-cum-Selection Committee and the Appointment Committee of the Cabinet (hereinafter referred to as 'ACC').

(c) The appointment of Respondent No. 4, a Chairman of SEBI, is mala fide.

3. Mr. Prashant Bhushan, learned Counsel appearing for the Petitioner, has made detailed submissions with regard to the manipulations and the maneuvers indulged in by the Petitioner with the active connivance of some other persons to successfully mislead the Search Committee as well as the ACC. He has highlighted that the Petitioner does not fulfill the requirements of Section 4(5) of SEBI Act

Held while dismissing the appeal,

the anxiety of these Business Houses for the removal of the present Chairman of SEBI is not wholly unimaginable. We make the aforesaid observations only to put on record that the present petition could have been dismissed as not maintainable for a variety of reasons. However, we have chosen to examine the entire issue to satisfy our judicial conscience that the appointment to such a High Powered Position has actually been made fairly and in accordance with the procedure established by law.

64. We find no merit in this petition which is accordingly dismissed.

XX

Tata Consultancy Services ltd vs Cyrus Investments Pvt Ltd and Ors., 2021

Relevant Sections:

SECURITIES AND EXCHANGE BOARD OF INDIA ACT, 1992 - Section 15 D (b); SECURITIES AND EXCHANGE BOARD OF INDIA ACT, 1992 - Section 15 E

Equivalent Citation: [2021]227CompCas1(SC), (2021)2CompLJ348(SC), MANU/SC/0227/2021

Number of pages in the Original Judgement:9

Case Note:

Company - Chairman - Removal of - - Two companies forming part of one group acquired reference shares and equity shares of Appellant - Father of Respondent No.11 was Non-Executive Director on Board of Appellant - By Resolution, Board of Directors of Appellant redesignated Respondent No.11 as its Executive Chairman - By another resolution, Board of Directors of Appellant replaced Respondent No.11 with Respondent No.2 as interim Non-Executive Chairman - Certain things happened and by separate Resolutions passed, Respondent No.11 was removed from Directorship of companies - Thereafter, complainant-companies filed company petition before National Company Law Tribunal on grounds of unfair prejudice, oppression and mismanagement - NCLT heard company petition on merits and dismissed same - Challenging order of NCLT, complainant companies filed appeal before Appellate Tribunal which was allowed - NCLAT held that proceedings of sixth meeting of Board of Directors of Appellant so far as it relates to removal and other actions taken against Respondent no. 11 was declared illegal and was set aside - NCLAT further held that Respondent and nominee of shall desist from taking any decision and decision of the Registrar of Companies changing Company from Public Company to Private Company was declared illegal and set aside - Hence, present appeal - Whether reliefs granted and directions issued by Appellate Tribunal, including reinstatement of Respondent No.11 into Board of Appellant, desist Respondent from taking any decision and decision of Registrar of Companies changing Company from Public Company to Private Company was suffer from any perversity.

Brief Facts:

The two companies acquired preference shares and equity shares of the paid-up share capital of Appellant. The father of Respondent No. 11 was a Non-Executive Director on the Board of appellant. The Respondent No. 11 was appointed as a Non-Executive Director on the Board. By a Resolution of the Board of Directors of Appellant, Respondent No. 11 was appointed as Executive Deputy Chairman. By a Resolution, the Board of Directors of Appellant company redesignated Respondent No. 11as its Executive Chairman. By a Resolution passed, the Board of Directors of appellant replaced Respondent No. 11 with Respondent No.2 as the interim Non-Executive Chairman. As a follow up, certain things happened and by separate Resolutions passed at the meetings of the shareholders of appellant. The Respondent No. 11 then resigned from the Directorship of a few other operating companies. Thereafter, complainant companies filed a company petition before the National Company Law Tribunal under Sections 241 and 242 read with 244 of the Companies Act, 2013, on the grounds of unfair prejudice, oppression and mismanagement. NCLT held the main company petition to be not maintainable at the instance of persons holding just around two percent of the issued share capital. The complainant companies filed appeals before NCLAT. These appeals were allowed granting waiver of the requirement of Section 244(1)(a) and remanding the matter back to NCLT for disposal on merits. Thereafter, NCLT heard the company petition on merits and dismissed the same. Challenging the order of the NCLT, the two complainant companies filed one appeal. The NCLAT held that the proceedings of the sixth meeting of the Board of Directors of appellant so far as it relates to removal and other actions taken against 11th Respondent was declared illegal and was set aside. As a sequel thereto, the person who had been appointed as Executive Chairman in place of 11th Respondent, his consequential appointment was declared illegal. The second Respondent and the nominee shall desist from taking any decision in advance which requires majority decision of the Board of Directors or in the Annual General Meeting. The decision of the Registrar of Companies changing the Company from Public Company to Private Company was declared illegal and set aside.

Held, while allowing the appeal:

(i) In any event the removal of a person from the post of Executive Chairman could not be termed as oppressive or prejudicial. The original cause of action for the complainant companies to approach NCLT was the removal of Respondent No.11 from the post of Executive Chairman. Though the complainant companies padded up their actual grievance with various historical facts to make a deceptive appearance, the causa proxima for the complaint was the removal of Respondent No.11 from the office of Executive Chairman. His removal from Directorship happened subsequent to the filing of the original complaint and that too for valid and justifiable reasons and hence NCLAT could not have laboured so much on the removal of Respondent No.2, for granting relief under Sections 241 and 242. [16.42]

(ii) The Appellant was a principal investment holding Company, of which the majority shareholding is with philanthropic Trusts. The majority shareholders were not individuals or corporate entities having deep pockets into which the dividends find their way if the Company does well and declares dividends. The dividends that the Trusts get are to find their way eventually to the fulfilment of charitable purposes. Therefore, NCLAT should have raised the most fundamental question whether it would be equitable to wind up the Company and thereby starve to death those charitable Trusts, especially on the basis of un-charitable allegations of oppressive and prejudicial conduct. Therefore, the finding of NCLAT that the facts otherwise justify the winding up of the Company under the just and equitable clause, was completely flawed. [16.54]

(iii) The Tribunal should always keep in mind the purpose for which remedies are made available under these provisions, before granting relief or issuing directions. It was on the touchstone of the objective behind these provisions that the correctness of the four reliefs granted by the Tribunal should be tested. If so done, it would be clear that NCLAT could not have granted the reliefs of reinstatement of Respondent No.2, restriction on the right to invoke Article 75(iii) restraining Respondent No.11 and the Nominee Directors from taking decisions in advance and setting aside the conversion of appellant into a private company. [17.35]

(iv) It should be pointed out that the complainant companies did not make a grievance out of Article 75 on the ground that it had been misused in the past and that such misuse tantamount to conduct oppressive or prejudicial to the interests of some of the members. The sine qua non for invoking Section 241 was that the affairs of the Company should have been conducted or are being conducted in a manner oppressive or prejudicial to some of the members. No single instance even of invocation of Article 75, leave alone misuse, was averred in the main company petition or in the application for amendment. Therefore, NCLAT could not have and should not have made Article 75 completely ineffective by passing an order of restraint. [18.3]

(v) NCLAT had agreed, on first principles, that it has no jurisdiction to declare any of the Articles of Association illegal. After having set a benchmark correctly, NCLAT neutralised Article 75 merely on the basis of likelihood of misuse. Section 241(1)(a) provides for a remedy, only in respect of past and present conduct or past and present continuous conduct. NCLAT had stretched Section 241(1)(a) to cover the likelihood of a future bad conduct, which was impermissible in law. [18.4]

(vi) Therefore, the order of NCLAT tinkering with the power available under Article 75 of the Articles of Association was wholly unsustainable. [18.11]

(vii) Objections were raised about Respondent No.2 vetting the minutes of the meetings of the Board post facto and his participation as a shadow Director. But Respondent No.11 himself sought, while accepting the office of Executive Chairmanship, the continued guidance of Respondent No.2. When the Board, of which Respondent No.11 was a Chairman, nominated Respondent no.2 as Chairman Emeritus and recorded their desire to look forward to his support and guidance, it was not open to the complainant companies to call Respondent no.2 a shadow Director. If someone, aggrieved after his removal from office could engage in shadow-boxing through the companies controlled by him, he could not accuse the very same person who chose him as successor to be a shadow director. Someone who gained entry through the very same door, could not condemn it when asked to exit. [19.37]

(viii) The challenge to the affirmative voting rights and the allegations revolving around pre consultation and pre clearance by the Trusts of all items in the agenda and Respondent No.2's indirect or direct influence or grip over the Board were all liable to be rejected. [19.38]

(ix) Placing reliance upon Section 163 of the Companies Act, 2013, it was contended that proportionate representation was statutorily recognised. But this argument was completely misconceived. Section 163 of the 2013 Act corresponds to Section 265 of the 1956 Act. It enables a company to provide in their Articles of Association, for the appointment of not less than two-thirds of the total number of Directors in accordance with the principle of proportionate representation by means of a single transferable vote. First of all, proportionate representation by means of a single transferable vote, was not the same as representation on the Board for a group of minority shareholders, in proportion to the percentage of shareholding they have. It was a system where the voters exercise their franchise by ranking several candidates of their choice, with first preference, second preference etc. Moreover, it was only an enabling provision and it was upto the company to make a provision for the same in their Articles, if they so choose. There was no statutory compulsion to incorporate such a provision. [19.50]

(x) NCLAT was completely wrong in holding as though Appellant, in connivance with the Registrar of companies did something clandestinely, contrary to the procedure established by law. The request made by appellant and the action taken by the Registrar of Companies to amend the Certificate of Incorporation were perfectly in order. [20.40]

(xi) Once the company had become a deemed public company, the privileges of a private company stood withdrawn and the company was entitled in law to allow renunciation of shares under rights issue. In any case, the validity of what was done was not in question. That they accepted deposits from public was the reason why they were not reconverted as a private company at that time. Once a new definition of the expression private company came into force under Section 2(68) of the 2013 Act, the only test to be applied was to find out if the company fits into the scheme under the new Act or not. This court need not go to the circulars issued by the department or the RBI when statutory provisions show the path with clarity. The description of the company in the forms filed under Rule 10, reflected the true position that prevailed then and they would not act as estoppel when the company was entitled to take advantage of the law. That the ability of the company to raise funds had now gone and that the company would have to repay the investments made by insurance companies, are all matters which the shareholders and the Directors are to take care. The question before the court was whether the reconversion was in accordance with law or not. The question was not whether it was good for the company or not. [20.42]

VIDEOS & TV SHOWS ON LAW & EXIM

List of some important videos & TV shows on Law & EXIM by Adv. Jayprakash Somani on his YouTube Channel 'Jayprakash Somani EXIM & Legal'

Legal Videos: Hindi -English

1) SLP in Supreme Court / Special Leave Petitions in the Supreme Court of India

2) Transfer of Civil & Criminal Cases by the Supreme Court of India / Transfer of Matrimonial Cases

3) Appellate Jurisdiction of the Supreme Court of India

4) Jurisdictions of the Supreme Court of India

5) Public Interest Litigation in the Supreme Court of India / PIL in Supreme Court

6) Article 32 Writ Petitions in the Supreme Court of India

7) Bail Matters Top 10 Supreme Court Cases

8) FIR Quashing in High Court & Supreme Court

9) Bail & Anticipatory Bail Matters in Supreme Court

10) Insolvency & Bankruptcy Matters in the Supreme Court

11) Insolvency & Bankruptcy Code 2016 Part 1

12) Insolvency & Bankruptcy Code 2016 Part 2

13) Insolvency & Bankruptcy Code 2016 Part 3

14) Corporate Liquidation Process

15) Supreme Court Rules & Procedures Webinar of 2.5 hour on Zoom

16) RDDBFI Act, 1993 (Introduction)

17) The Indian Contact Act 1872

18) Negotiable Instruments Act (Introduction)

19) How to avoid matrimonial disputes& some more videos

20)SEBI Matters in the Supreme Court

21) Matrimonial Matters: Supreme Court's 20 Case Laws

22) Consumer Matters Supreme Court's 20 Case Laws

23) Service Matters Supreme Court's 20 Case Laws

24) How to Search Lawyer for Your Matter

25) Property Matters Supreme Court's 20 Case Laws

26) Bail Matters: Supreme Court's 20 Case Laws

27) Supreme Court / High Court Vacation Benches

28)69000 Teacher's Recruitment Matters of UP Government in the Supreme Court

29) Contempt of Court Matters in the Supreme Court

30) Advocate Act's Matters in the Supreme Court

31) Business Law Matters in the Supreme Court

32) Banking Matters in the Supreme Court

33) Labour Law Matters in the Supreme Court

34) Arbitration Matters in the Supreme Court

35) Careers in Law -Zoom Webinar by Adv. Jayprakash Somani

36) Civil Matters in the Supreme Court

37) Consumer Protection Act | Consumer Matters in the Supreme Court

38) Corporate Matters in the Supreme Court

39) Criminal Matters in the Supreme Court

40) Role of Respondent in the Supreme Court of India

41) Motor Vehicle Accident Matters in Supreme Court with case laws

42) Article 131 Original Suits in Supreme Court

43)PIL in Supreme Court/ Public Interest Litigations in the Supreme Court of India'

44)CAB Citizenship Amendment Bill is not Unconstitutional

45) Supreme Court of India Cases & Process – Marathi

46) Legal Services Export / Export of Legal Services

47) Transfer of Matrimonial Cases by the Supreme Court of India

48) Public Interest Litigation PIL

49) The Specific Relief Act (Introduction)

50) Corporate Insolvency Resolution Process CIRP

51)ABMM's Career 5 - Careers in Law

52) Transfer of cases by Supreme Court

53) Writ Petitions in High Court & Supreme Court of India

54) Supreme Court Jurisdictions - Appeals, SLP, Writ Petitions, Transfer, Original, Review, Curative

55)LEGAL INDIA TV Show: Cases Handled in Supreme Court

56) Corporate Liquidation Process

57) Legal Services Export / Export of Legal Services

EXIM Videos: Hindi -English

1) Yes, I can do Import Export Business Easily! 36 points excellent video in Hindi

2) Yes, I can do Import Export Business Easily! 36 points excellent video in English

3) Import Export Business – Hindi video

4) Import Export Business - English video

5) Export Import Marathi TV Interview

6) Scope for Commerce Students in International Business- TV Show

7) Scope for Management Student in International Business- TV Show

8) Scope for Engineering Students in International Business – TV Show

9) Women in International Business- TV Show

10) How to do Import Export Business Successfully!‘

11) Where one can get full information on Import Export Business?

12) What to do import & export?

13) Import Export Workshop/ Training/Course/ Diploma

14) How to Start Import Export Business & How to grow it. Live Webinar

15) Success Stories & Failure Stories in Import & Export Business

16) For MSME Scope in Export & Import...

17) Exports In Agri. & Food Products – English & some more videos

18) Exports to Dubai, Aabudhabii. e. UAE

19) Jewelry Exports from India

20) How to attend EXIM workshop to become excellent Exporter

21) Import Export Best Training Course – Online & Offline

22) Agri Product Export

23) Scope for Woman in International Business

24) Management Graduates Scope in International Business

25) Pharma Product's Export

26) Best Import Export Course | Practical Training | Aaronica Global Exim

27) Import Export Business for Commerce Graduates

28) How Do I Get Export Orders? Finding International Buyers

29) What Is APEDA In Import Export Business?

30) Which Is The Best Product To Export From India?

31)EXIM Remark by Manoj Kumar Faridabad

32)EXIM Remarks by Mahesh Telangana

33) What Licenses I Need To Start Import/ Export?

34) How Can I Increase My Import Export Business?

35) Which Is Best B2B Website For Import/Export Business?

36) Export Import Management with Global Marketing

37) How to Start Export Import Business | 51 Points Video

38) Scope for Commerce & Other Graduates in International Business

39)BE A SUCCESSFUL EXPORTER FOR OUR NATION - Marathi video

40) Export of Textile , Cotton, Agri., Food, & other products & services

41) Exports from MP, CG, MH, GJ & CA in Fresh Fruits & Vegetables

42) Exports in Agri. & Food Products- Hindi

43) Start your Online/E-Commerce Business

44) How to Start Export Import Business & Grow it

45) Exports in Textile & Other Products

46) Start and grow EXIM business - Live English Webinar

47)'Import Export Business!' Why, Who, What & How can one do it easily!!

48) Live: Export of Product & Services During & After Lock Down Period

49) Frauds in Import Export Business

50) Import Export for Business Man

51) Import & Export for Women

51) Import & Export for Graduate & Post - Graduate Students

52) Agriculture Exports from India

53) Digital Marketing Setup - Marathi

54)2nd Secret of Successful Businessman

55) Digital Marketing Set up

56) Legal Services Export / Export of Legal Services

57) Export & Import with UAE

58) Service Exports / Exports by Service Providers

59) Import Export Workshop/ Training/Course/ Diploma

60) Exports & Imports with USA

61) Selection on Product for Export

62) Top Products Exported from India

63) What to do import & export?

64)ABMM Career 2 - 'Careers in Business & Industries

65) How to do Import Export Business Successfully!'

66)5 Secrets of Successful Businessman

67) Export from MP, Chhattisgarh & Vidarbha Nagpur

68)EXIM Hindi - Textile & Apparel Export

69)EXIM Hindi - Export Import Practical Training In Delhi, Kolkata, Mumbai and Pune

70) Import Export Business

71) Import Export Business Hindi

72) Import Export Business English video

73) Import Export Business Marathi

74) Women in International Business by Exim Guru Adv. Jayprakash Somani

75) Opportunities in Foreign Trade- Adv. Jayprakash Somani's special interview

List Of Adv. Jayprakash Somani's Books

1. Supreme Court of India's Leading Case Laws on 'Insolvency & Bankruptcy Code 2016'

2. Bail Matters – Supreme Court's Latest Leading Case Laws

3. Arbitration Matters- Supreme Court's Latest Leading Case Laws

4. Property Matters - Supreme Court's Latest Leading Case Laws

5. Matrimonial Matters- Supreme Court's Latest Leading Case Laws

6. Election Matters- Supreme Court's Latest Leading Case Laws

7.SEBI Matters- Supreme Court's Latest Leading Case Laws

8. Banking Matters- Supreme Court's Latest Leading Case Laws

9. Service Matters- Supreme Court's Latest Leading Case Laws

10. Contempt of Court Matters- Supreme Court's Latest Leading Case Laws

11. Consumer Protection Matters- Supreme Court's Latest Leading Case Laws

12. Corporate Law- Supreme Court's Latest Leading Case Laws

13. Supreme Court's AOR Exam- Leading Cases

14. Armed Force Tribunal - Supreme Court's Latest Leading Case Laws

15. Acquittal From 376 - Supreme Court's Latest Leading Case Laws

16. Negotiable instrument – Supreme Court's Latest Leading Case Laws

17. Contract Act- Supreme Court's Latest Leading Case Laws

18. INSIDER TRADING AND MARKET MANIPULATION- SEBI ACT - Supreme Court's Leading Case Laws

19. Foreign Exchange and Management Act- Supreme Court's Latest Leading Case Laws

20. Income Tax Act- Supreme Court's Latest Leading Case Laws

21. Company Law- Supreme Court's Latest Leading Case Laws

22. Competition & Monopoly Matters- Supreme Court's Latest Leading Case Laws

23. Compassionate Appointment- Service Matters- Supreme Court's Latest Leading Case Laws

24. Compulsory Retirement- Service Matters- Supreme Court's Latest Leading Case Laws

25. Voluntary Retirement- Service Matters- Supreme Court's Latest Leading Case Laws

26. Removal/Dismissal/Termination from Service- Supreme Court's Latest Leading Case Laws

27. Seniority- Service Matter- Supreme Court's Latest Leading Case Laws

28. Promotion- Service Matter- Supreme Court's Latest Leading Case Laws

29. Equal Pay for Equal Work- Service Matter- Supreme Court's Latest Leading Case Laws

30. Condition of Service- Service Matter- Supreme Court's Latest Leading Case Laws

31. Customs Act- Supreme Court's Leading Case Laws

32. Information Technology Act- Supreme Court's Latest Leading Case Laws

These Books are available online at

1. **Notion Press:** https://notionpress.com/author/jayprakash_somani
2. **Amazon:** https://www.amazon.in/s?k=jayprakash+somani
3. **Flipkart:** https://www.flipkart.com/search?q=Jayprakash%20Somani

Printed by Libri Plureos GmbH in Hamburg,
Germany